WM. NEWTON CLARKE
AND
POSTCONSERVATIVE EVANGELICALISM

WM. NEWTON CLARKE
AND
POSTCONSERVATIVE EVANGELICALISM

&

A MODEL MINI-DISSERTATION
FOR
STUDENTS OF CHRISTIAN THOUGHT

MAX H. SOTAK, PH.D.

Sotakoff
Publishing

WM. NEWTON CLARKE AND POSTCONSERVATIVE EVANGELICALISM
A Model Mini-Dissertation for Students of Christian Thought
Max H. Sotak

ISBN-10: 0-9896808-5-1
ISBN-13: 978-0-9896808-5-1

Published by: Sotakoff Publishing

Back Cover: The twin towers of Zwingli's Grossmünster church in Zurich

WM. NEWTON CLARKE
AND
POSTCONSERVATIVE EVANGELICALISM

ABSTRACT

The purpose of this study is to assess the experiential theology of William Newton Clarke as an instrumental case of contemporary postconservative evangelicalism. Relying primarily on Clarke's *Outline of Christian Theology* and contemporary statements of postconservative evangelicalism, the study pursues five objectives: (1) To analyze Clarke's experiential theology as a mediation of the influences of 19th Century liberalism and evangelicalism in an early 20th Century context; (2) To assess Clarke's *Outline* as a unique contribution to Christian thought; (3) To compare and contrast Clarke's experiential theology with contemporary evangelical postconservatives; (4) To evaluate postconservativism as a paradigm case of the movement of modern theology from *Dogmatik* to *Glaubenslehre*; (5) To propose adjustments to Clarke's theology to enhance his personal relevance. The conclusion of the study is that Clarke's theology fits the distinctives of postconservative evangelicalism, identifying him as an authentic and relevant resource for these Christians.

KEY WORDS

ACTIVISM: The fourth hallmark of postconservative evangelicalism that refers to evangelism and social transformation as means of seeking the kingdom of God (Olson, 2011:175).

BIBLICISM: The second hallmark of postconservative evangelicalism that refers to a commitment to the authority of the Bible "in all matters of faith and practice" (Olson, 2011:172-173). Not to be confused with a biblicism that accepts no truth as Christian except what is taken from the Bible "in its literal meaning" (Harvey, 1964:44).

CHRISTOMONISM: A term associated with Karl Barth that goes beyond the idea that Jesus Christ is central to theology

(Christocentrism) by affirming that all Christian knowledge has a Christological basis, thereby excluding any natural knowledge of God outside of Christ (Ramm, 1966:24).

CONDITIONAL IMMORTALITY: The view that immortality is not "an intrinsic property of the soul" but a divine gift of Christ received in salvation (Harvey, 1964:56).

CONVERSIONISM: The first hallmark of postconservative evangelicalism that refers to "a belief in and spiritual experience of conversion to Christ by faith," which is grounded in a work of God within the life of a person (Olson, 2011:170-172).

CRUCICENTRISM: The third hallmark of postconservative evangelicalism that refers to "piety centered on Jesus Christ and his atoning death" (Olson, 2011:173-175).

DOGMATIK: A German word meaning "dogmatic theology," which is used to describe an official expression of Christian theology that is distilled from biblical propositions and organized into an essentially deductive system of Christian beliefs or dogmas.

EVANGELICAL LIBERALISM: An expression of Christianity centered in Christ, committed to the essence of historic Christianity, and seeking a theology believable by intelligent moderns (Cauthen, 1983:27-29).

EXPERIENTIAL THEOLOGY: The intellectual expression of the scientific study of religion—religion being defined by a spiritual experience involving the whole person, especially the will and affections: "Theology is preceded by religion, as botany by the life of plants" (Clarke, 1898:4, 1).

GLAUBENSLEHRE: A German word meaning "doctrine of faith," which is used to describe an expression of Christian theology that acknowledges the historical relativity and subjective transparency of the church's and the individual's reflection on the revelation of God—but not necessarily to the extremes of relativism, historicism, or anti-supernaturalism (Allen, 1980:41; Gerrish, 1993).

INSTRUMENTAL CASE STUDY: A qualitative research method that employs a unique or interesting case to illustrate and illuminate the generalizations of an explanatory theory (Grandy, 2010:473-475).

POSTCONSERVATIVE EVANGELICALISM (PCE): A definition of evangelicalism that represents a theological system focused on a "centered set" of four "hallmarks" plus one additional commitment: conversionism, Biblicism, crucicentrism, activism, and respect for historic Christian orthodoxy (Olson, 2011:163, 168, 168-175).

ACKNOWLEDGEMENTS

This mini-dissertation was originally submitted to North-West University of South Africa (Potchefstroom Campus) for the degree of Master of Theology (M.Th.) in Church and Dogma History (conferred 2016). The study was pursued under the direction of Drs. Daniel Lioy and Nico Vorster. My special thanks to Dr. Vorster of the Faculty of Theology (School of Human Sciences) for his patient review and critical perspective, especially on the finer theoretical details of the study. Sincere thanks are also due to Drs. Gary Dorrien and Roger Olson who expressed their interest in this study and offered positive comments on its central argument.

HOW TO USE THIS MINI-DISSERTATION

This mini-dissertation was designed for use as a companion to the author's foundational work, *Evangelical Belief: A Course Guide to Christian Thought* (Sotak, 2017). *Evangelical Belief* provides a robust course of study designed to prepare the student for a scholarly thesis or capstone project in Christian thought. The instrumental case study is one of the most effective research methods to facilitate learning in the fields of philosophy, theology, and apologetics. Three chapters in *Evangelical Belief* provide concise examples of the instrumental case study (14, 37, 38), and the section on methodology below (1.4) goes into more detail on how this method works. The correlation between ideas and their embodiment in movements and individuals is at the heart of Christian thought, and a good model takes the mystery out of organizing and documenting our learning. I have found this qualitative research method to be the most enjoyable and attainable study method for comparing Christian thinkers and theories. My hope is that this model will be useful to your own scholarly endeavors.

TABLE OF CONTENTS

1.0 INTRODUCTION

1.1 BACKGROUND & PROBLEM STATEMENT

1.1.1 BACKGROUND

William Newton Clarke (1841-1912) claims the distinction of having produced the first systematic theology of American liberalism and of having mediated both evangelicalism and liberalism within the early 20th Century context (Dorrien, 2003:31-42; Handy, 1980:84). His own work and the scholarly reflection on him reveals a creative thinker who came to theology late in life and combined evangelical piety with the basic principles of Ritschlean liberalism (Clarke, 1896, 1898, 1899a, 1899b, 1900a, 1900b, 1901, 1903a, 1903b, 1905, 1909a, 1909b, 1911a, 1911b; Dalton, 1903; Knox, 1908; Brown, 1910; Clarke, 1916; Tinsley, 1917; Howe, 1963, 1980; Cochran, 1962: Reist, 1970, 1975; Tull, 1972; Handy, 1980, Dorrien, 2003; Garrett, 2009). Cauthen (1983:27, 5-25) would classify Clarke as an "evangelical liberal" who embraced the liberal principles of continuity, autonomy, and dynamism. These principles were inspired by the doctrine of evolution, which prepared the way for liberal theologies controlled by the belief in the immanence of God in natural processes (1983:7). While Clarke himself was "a person of one book" and made little direct use of German theology or Higher Criticism, his view of the Bible developed over sixty years as he negotiated the theological "crisis" of the 19th Century (Dorrien, 2003:31).

A careful study of Clarke reveals a Christian theologian who is obviously more evangelical than liberal and who, like his contemporary A. H. Strong, emphasized immanence "but not at the expense of transcendence" (Reist, 1970:35, 39). Christian supernaturalism is not compromised in his theology, even though in some areas "immanence is the dominating characteristic." In appraising Clarke's significance to

13

contemporary theologians, it is possible to see his own theological autobiography, *Sixty Years With the Bible*, as a "postconservative" testimony ahead of its time (Clarke, 1909b; Olson, 2007, 2011). This autobiography combined with Clarke's (1898) pivotal work on systematic theology, *An Outline of Christian Theology*, offers a unique opportunity to probe the subjective motivations behind a personal statement of Christian belief that resonates with contemporary discussions on the definition of evangelicalism. Could it be that William Newton Clarke, the author of America's first evangelical liberal theology text, is also a prototypical postconservative evangelical?

In assessing the relationship between William Newton Clarke and postconservative evangelicalism, a subsidiary question arises about the movement of modern theology. If it can be shown that Clarke may be considered a precursor and instrumental case of postconservative evangelicalism, does this also mean that these evangelicals illustrate what Brian Gerrish (1993:239-248) describes as the movement of modern theology from *Dogmatik* to *Glaubenslehre*? In simple terms, *Dogmatik* refers to theology as a deductive system of biblically derived dogmas, and *Glaubenslehre* refers to theology as an inductive study of historically rooted beliefs. While this question is subsidiary, it is historically significant and serves to place this study within the larger context of modern theology since Schleiermacher.

The primary motivation for this study is the personal relevance of William Newton Clarke. This researcher has found Clarke's *Outline* to be one of the most engaging and edifying theology texts encountered in four decades of theological study. Postconservative evangelicalism's centered set of five hallmarks "are not boundary markers but landmarks, not sides of a box but foci of attention and action" (Olson, 2011:175). Earlier expressions of essentially the same approach were termed "critical orthodoxy" by Leith (1981:31) and "progressive orthodoxy" in the 19th Century (The Editors of "The Andover Review", 1886). While it will be argued that Clarke's theology fits this definition of evangelicalism, there are also points at which the theology of Clarke could be adjusted to improve his appeal to this researcher. Therefore, a subsidiary concern of this study will be to propose adjustments to Clarke's theology that will enhance his personal relevance.

1.1.2 PROBLEM STATEMENT

The primary research question may now be stated: In what ways, if any, is the experiential theology of William Newton Clarke an authentic and relevant resource for contemporary "postconservative" evangelicals?

The questions that arise from the research question are as follows:

> To what extent, if any, is Clarke's experiential theology a mediation of 19th Century liberalism and evangelicalism in an early 20th Century context?
>
> In what ways is Clarke's *Outline of Christian Theology* a unique contribution to Christian theology based on his experiential method?
>
> What are some potential similarities and differences between Clarke's experiential theology and that of contemporary evangelical postconservatives?
>
> To what extent, if any, is postconservatism a paradigm case of the movement of modern theology from *Dogmatik* to *Glaubenslehre*?
>
> In what ways might Clarke's theology be adjusted to enhance its personal relevance?

1.2   THE AIM & OBJECTIVES

1.2.1   THE AIM

The main aim of this thesis is to assess the theology of William Newton Clarke as an instrumental case of contemporary "postconservative" evangelicalism.

1.2.2   THE OBJECTIVES

The specific objectives of this study are as follows:

> To analyze Clarke's experiential theology as a mediation of the influences of 19th Century liberalism and evangelicalism in an early 20th Century context.

> To assess Clarke's *Outline of Christian Theology* as a unique contribution to Christian thought based on his experiential method.

> To compare and contrast Clarke's experiential theology with contemporary evangelical postconservatives.

> To evaluate postconservatism as a paradigm case of the movement of modern theology from *Dogmatik* to *Glaubenslehre*.

> To propose adjustments to Clarke's theology to enhance its personal relevance.

1.3   CENTRAL THEORETICAL ARGUMENT

The central theoretical argument of this thesis is that the experiential theology of William Newton Clarke remains an authentic and relevant resource for postconservative evangelicals. A preliminary review of Clarke's understanding of Christian doctrine reflects a closer alignment with the hallmarks of postconservative evangelicalism than with any other contemporary definition, and his own theological progress from within the context of conservative evangeli-

calism mirrors the trajectory of contemporary postconservatives, such as Roger Olson (2011), Clark Pinnock
(1990b), Stanley Grenz (1993), and Donald Bloesch (1978,
1985). The fact that Clarke travelled a similar path a century earlier strongly suggests his relevance to the current
debate over the definition of evangelicalism.

1.4 METHODOLOGY

This study is done from within the Evangelical Protestant
tradition. An authoritative statement of evangelical faith is
offered by the National Association of Evangelicals (NAE,
2009):

> We believe the Bible to be the inspired, the
> only infallible, authoritative Word of God.

> We believe that there is one God, eternally
> existent in three persons: Father, Son and
> Holy Spirit.

> We believe in the deity of our Lord Jesus
> Christ, in His virgin birth, in His sinless
> life, in His miracles, in His vicarious and
> atoning death through His shed blood, in
> His bodily resurrection, in His ascension to
> the right hand of the Father, and in His
> personal return in power and glory.

> We believe that for the salvation of lost and
> sinful people, regeneration by the Holy
> Spirit is absolutely essential.

> We believe in the present ministry of the
> Holy Spirit by whose indwelling the Chris-
> tian is enabled to live a godly life.

> We believe in the resurrection of both the
> saved and the lost; they that are saved unto
> the resurrection of life and they that are
> lost unto the resurrection of damnation.

> We believe in the spiritual unity of believ-
> ers in our Lord Jesus Christ.

The instrumental case study is the proper research method for this study, as opposed to an intrinsic or collective case study (cf. Sotak, 2008:10-14). As a qualitative research method, this case study focuses on unique rather than typical examples (Stake, 1995:8). Generalizations derived from a theoretical model are brought to the case, and the case illustrates and illuminates what is overlooked in typical cases (1995:4). Thus, the theology of William Newton Clarke serves the instrumental goal of illustrating and illuminating the generalizations of postconservatism. As a single exemplar, Clarke presents a unique perspective, which emphasizes "richness rather than generalizability" (Grandy, 2010:475; Stake, 1995:3-4). Whereas a collective case study illustrates general issues through several instrumental cases, the instrumental case study illuminates those issues by their embodiment in a unique and interesting individual. The richness of Clarke's perspective as a central feature of the study warrants viewing the study as both an intrinsic and instrumental case study, but the instrumental goal is primary (Grandy, 2010:474). Grandy captures the value and appeal of this methodology: "The key in both the intrinsic and instrumental case study is the opportunity to learn."

The "issues" of postconservatism provide a powerful conceptual structure for organizing a study of William Newton Clarke (Stake, 1995:17, 20). Since the study of historical theology is a complex interaction between the issues raised by theoretical models and individual theologians, the instrumental case study would seem to be one of the best methods available to students of theology. The qualitative narrative leads the reader to an experiential understanding of the case (1995:41). Given the depth and detail of Clarke's theology, we would expect this outcome. Specifically, the study should confirm the "patterns" and "consistencies" in the theology of Clarke predicted by the postconservative model of Roger Olson, leading to "vicarious experience" (1995:44, 48). Therefore, the study should be judged by the extent to which the theology of Clarke and the postconservative model illuminate and engage the reader.

"Correspondence" is the appropriate method to validate the observations and assertions of the study, and "pattern consistency" defines the meaning of correspondence (Stake, 1995:78). In the context of this study, the theoretical model defines pattern consistency: "Often the patterns will be known in advance, drawn from the research questions, serving as a template for the analysis" (1995:78). The basic procedure, then, will be to look for the conceptual patterns of the model to reappear within the case. As the "centered set" of postconservative commitments are noted in connection with Clarke's theological method, the validity of the observations of the study will be established (Olson, 2011:163-164).

The triangulation of data also requires a distinction between the theoretical model and the case. Stake (1995:112-114) refers to the following protocols: data source, investigator, theory, and methodological triangulation. Clearly, theory triangulation fits both the theoretical model of postconservatism and the theological method of Clarke. Stake (1995:113) describes how this protocol works when several investigators compare their findings: "To the extent they describe the phenomenon with similar detail, the description is triangulated. To the extent they agree on its meaning the interpretation is triangulated." Provided that postconservatism has received a clear statement that is recognized among reputable evangelical authorities, the theoretical model may be triangulated by the consensus of the experts. Triangulating the case requires observation, document review, and correspondence. A single-case study based on a literary record offers an opportunity to explore the thought of a unique and creative theologian. Given an appropriate theoretical model, these methods will be sufficient to validate the observations and assertions related to Clarke's theology.

With respect to epistemological method, Stake (1995) raises some important issues for the evangelical theologian. He contends that most qualitative research proceeds on the belief that knowledge is "constructed rather than discovered" (1995:99). Stake's commitment to experiential knowledge reflects an underlying relativism that seems to confer equal validity to all interpretations (1995:104). Fortunately, he recognizes that not all interpretations are equal, some proving themselves more credible and useful (1995:102). Credibility does not refer to a correspondence with reality, however, since he believes such correspondence cannot be tested (1995:101).

In this researcher's view, Stake's version of constructivism does not escape relativism. One can affirm relativity without relativism within a critical realist epistemology. If, as Stake argues, pattern correspondences cannot be tested using a correspondence truth test, then there is simply no way for fact and interpretation to connect. Facts impact interpretations because correspondences may be tested as approximations at the very least. Relativity recognizes that the correspondence test is easier to apply to some facts than others, metaphysical statements being more difficult to test than statements about empirical facts. It will be granted that metaphysical statements require complex patterns of inference from experience, and these are not universally agreed upon. Thus, relativity complicates some issues, but denying the possibility of applying correspondence as a truth test seems to leave little basis for Stake's credibility criterion. Credibility and utility may be appealed to as complementary tests, but they must be grounded in reality if they are not to resolve in pragmatic relativism. Even as combined tests, utility would not seem to support credibility unless the practical results of utility map to an empirically fitting outcome and a normative *telos* or goal.

Stake (1995) recognizes the key weakness of his constructivism: "The stronger one's belief in constructed reality, the more difficult it is to believe that any complex observation or interpretation can be triangulated" (1995:114). This admission confirms this researcher's persuasion that constructivism is ultimately self-refuting. The very statement of constructivism as an epistemological method founders on its own pragmatic relativism. The use of triangulation protocols to verify accurate interpretations requires that credibility be more than a subjective appeal and that utility satisfy more than a personal goal. If these criteria are to have meaning, they must connect—approximately at least—to the way things really are. It would seem reasonable, then, that critical realism with relativity provides a better alternative to the epistemological problems raised by qualitative research.

1.5 CONCLUSION

The appeal of an instrumental case study is the opportunity it provides to rediscover a unique and interesting theologian of the past by bringing his thought into contact with relevant issues of the present. The theology of William Newton Clarke deserves further attention in light of modern discussions of the definition of evangelicalism. Like postconservative evangelicals of today, Clarke was mediating the conservative and progressive trajectories of his time with a creativity and originality that established him as a pacesetter of American theology in the early 20th Century. This study proceeds, then, on the conviction that Clarke's theology likely has much to offer postconservatives who share his ecumenical vision for evangelical unity in a similar environment of change and Protestant plurality. It is not uncommon in the history of theology that the challenges of a new age are anticipated a century before by pioneers ahead of their time. Just as John Hus anticipated Luther by a century, so Clarke anticipates postconservatives by a century and offers an instructive example of how they might respond to an age seeking to mediate Christian faith, modernity, and postmodernity.

2.0 REVIEW OF THE LITERATURE

2.1 INTRODUCTION

The purpose of the literature review, according to Madsen (1992:62), is to present a "representative sample . . . of the *important* findings of relevant studies and theory." This definition stresses the importance of ideas more than authors, the "truly *germane* works" more than the body of all work on a subject. Therefore, the following review focuses attention on the findings of highest quality and relevance to the aim, objectives, and argument of the study.

With respect to the objectives of the study, the literature review must provide evidence of sufficient resources to fulfill those objectives. Specifically, the analysis of Clarke's experiential theology and his *Outline* requires an understanding of the scope and content of each of his works, and comparing, contrasting, and evaluating his theology in relation to postconservative evangelicalism requires an understanding of the authoritative representatives and tenets of the movement. Evaluating postconservatism as a paradigm case of the movement of modern theology from *Dogmatik* to *Glaubenslehre* is a more specialized question and requires authoritative and focused studies that define the issue clearly so that a sound judgment can be made.

2.2 LITERATURE ON CLARKE'S THEOLOGY

The theology of William Newton Clarke presents an appealing opportunity to study the mind and work of a great theologian. Not only did Clarke write the first American systematic theology of evangelical liberalism, but he also wrote supporting works that further explained the mature theology of his *Outline*. About a decade after his systematic theology was published in 1898, Clarke (1909b) traced the development of his thinking about the Bible over sixty years and the manner in which the Bible was to be used in theological reflection. He also delivered a series of published lectures at prestigious American institutions, such as Yale Divinity School, Johns Hopkins University, and the Harvard University School of Theology (Clarke, 1905, 1899a, 1899b). The scholarly impact of this work is noted by Howe (1980:23-24). Public recognition came through extensive publication on both sides of the Atlantic as well as honorary doctorates conferred by Yale University (1900, D.D.), Johns Hopkins University (1901, D.D.), and Columbia University (1910, S.T.D.). The final publication of Clarke's (1920) work was a collection of addresses that clarify the prominent themes of the *Outline*, such as immortality (1911, Yale Divinity School), mystery in religion (1896, Hamilton Theological Seminary), the atonement (1900, Haverford College), the relation of science to religion (1901, Oberlin College), revealed theology (1903, Harvard University), and the Christian ministry (1903, Andover Theological Seminary).

2.2.1 PRIMARY SOURCES ON CLARKE'S THEOLOGY

The wide acclaim and importance of Clarke's (1898) *Outline of Christian Theology* makes it the best primary source to consult for the purposes of this study. A number of supporting works are also critical to the clarification of his method and distinctive doctrines. Clarke's (1905:vii) Yale lectures, *The Use of the Scriptures in Theology*, are helpful in presenting the author's view of "the right using of the Bible in present conditions whether by students, by preachers, or by the people." These lectures anticipate Clarke's (1909b) theological autobiography, *Sixty Years With the Bible*, which provides personal insight into specific theological struggles and solutions reflected in the *Outline*. Clarke's (1909a) volume, *The Christian Doctrine of God*, while essentially in accord with the *Outline*, shows some movement in Clarke's thinking on the doctrine of the Trinity toward a more consistent application of his experiential method. This work is used primarily in proposing adjustments to Clarke's theology.

Clarke's (1899a, 1899b) two lecture series of 1899 also provide additional insight into issues treated in the *Outline*, especially with respect to the doctrine of God (1899a) and the "great contributions" of the Christian faith in the world (1899b:3-4). This second work elaborates Clarke's view of the essential elements of Christianity and serves as a popular digest of the heart of the *Outline*. More important than these two works is Clarke's (1920) last published work, *Immortality: A Study of Belief, and Other Addresses*. Clarke's (1911a) commitment to the doctrine of immortal soulism is defended in the first of these addresses, which was delivered at Yale Divinity School. This topic will be taken up in proposing adjustments to Clarke's theology, the address providing more apologetic support for the author's belief than does the *Outline*. A second address, *The Work of Christ For Our Salvation*, was delivered at Haverford College and provides additional insight into Clarke's precise position on the atonement, which was misunderstood by some critics who were unfamiliar with this obscure but important lecture (Clarke, 1900b).

2.2.2 SECONDARY SOURCES ON CLARKE'S THEOLOGY

The relevant secondary sources on Clarke are those required to confirm the importance of his contributions and their interpretation. Emily Clarke's biography of her husband collects testimonies of appreciation from a number of well-known students and colleagues, including Walter Rauchenbusch, D.C. Macintosh, Henry H. Peabody, Harry Emerson Fosdick, William Adams Brown, and several others (Clarke, 1916:124-125, 257-260, 170-184, 117-119,

185-210). Dorrien (2003:41) notes that William Adams Brown in particular was "unsurpassed in his affection and appreciation for Clarke" and loved his serenity in print and in person, his deep spirituality, and his relevance to the times. He admired Clarke's contemporary statement of old truths and believed that his theology preserved both intellectual integrity and traditional Christian beliefs. While there were not many scholarly responses to Clarke's work by 1920, Emily Clarke's collected materials from diaries, letters and testimonials provide a rich resource for understanding Clarke and his experiential theology (cf. Dalton, 1903; Knox, 1908; Brown, 1910; Tinsley, 1917).

Later scholarly work on Clarke, while not plentiful, is adequate to confirm a full understanding of his theology for the purpose of evaluating his congruence with postconservative evangelicalism. The most useful resource is Howe's (1980) published dissertation of 1959, *The Theology of William Newton Clarke: Systematic Theologian of Theological Liberalism* (cf. Cochran, 1962). This is a quality work that reflects careful attention to the details and nuances of Clarke's thought. Three less extensive treatments are also be useful in clarifying Clarke's thought by enabling a comparison of interpretations (Tull, 1972; Dorrien, 2003; Garrett, 2009). Three relevant periodicals also focus on the distinctives of Clarke's theology (Reist, 1970, 1975; Handy, 1980).

2.3 LITERATURE ON POSTCONSERVATISM

Given the aim of the study to assess the theology of Clarke as an instrumental case of postconservative evangelicalism, the goal was to discover which sources best represent and explain this contemporary movement within evangelicalism. While there are several excellent exemplars, the works by Olson (2007, 2011), Pinnock (1990b), and Pinnock and

Callen (2006) are the most useful for the purposes of the study. Given that the centerpiece of Clarke's theology and method is his *Outline*, it is necessary to identify postconservative works elaborating a similar approach. Of these, Olson's provides the most systematic treatment of a postconservative method. In addition, he identifies other postconservative authorities and major contributors, such as Pinnock (1990b), Grenz (1993), Knight (1997), and Collins (2005).

2.3.1 SOURCES ON POSTCONSERVATIVE METHOD

Olson's (2007) *Reformed and Always Reforming*, combined with his contribution to Naselli's and Hanson's (2011) *Four Views on the Spectrum of Evangelicalism*, addresses two important needs of this study. First, these sources provide the best current statement of a postconservative theological method by an American theologian who is recognized as a foremost authority on evangelicalism (cf. Olson, 2004). Second, Olson's (2007) main work provides a thorough coverage of all the issues of postconservatism and serves as a guide to other scholarly advocates of this approach and their publications. The thesis of the book is "simple but controversial: it is possible to be more evangelical by being less conservative" (2007:7). This central thesis of postconservatism seems to align—approximately at least—with the evangelical liberalism of Clarke and therefore provides presumptive evidence for the central theoretical argument of the study.

Central to the agenda of postconservatives is to escape their classification as "part of an evangelical left" (Olson, 2007:12; cf. Erickson, 1997:33). The problem here, according to Olson, is that the distinction between left and right is the product of enlightenment modernity and simply does not hold up in the face of a postmodern critique, which tends to reject dualisms. Moreover, the distinction serves to privilege the authority of tradition against legitimate criticism. Postconservatism, however, is seeking to escape "some of the conundrums and dead ends of traditional theology" without disregarding or disrespecting tradition (2007:12). These emphases also seem to be present in Clarke, who was not a typical liberal or conservative of his time. Given his current classification as an evangelical liberal, it would appear that the postconservative analysis would call that classification into question, and Olson's work provides the basis upon which such a case could be made. Further elaboration of postconservatism in relation to modern theology is provided by Pinnock (1990b), Gerrish (1993), and Allen (1980). While Olson describes the movement in its contemporary context, Pinnock extends the perspective backward to the 19th Century, the context in which Clarke lived and wrote. This broader historical perspective is also necessary to support an alignment between Clarke and postconservatism.

2.3.2 SOURCES ON POSTCONSERVATIVE BIBLIOLOGY

The inspiration and authority of the Bible is a hallmark of evangelicalism, and no alignment between Clarke and postconservatism can be justified apart from consideration of this issue. Much of Clarke's work was devoted to the use of the Bible, and postconservatives—like Clarke—also depart from what Erickson (2013:191) calls the "absolute" and Clarke (1898:35) calls the "complete" inerrancy position. While Clarke's (1898:10-46; 1905, 1909b) position on scripture is elaborated in three works, a comprehensive postconservative treatment is also needed to make the comparison. Pinnock and Callen (2006) provide the most extensive treatment of biblical authority from that perspective, and Fackre (1987:60-156) provides a comprehensive typology of options on authority to enable a precise classification of Clarke's views of biblical infallibility. The work by Pinnock and Callen is the contemporary counterpart to Clarke's (1905) book, *The Use of the Scriptures in Theology*, and Bloesch (1978:51-87; 1985) presents a theological method in line with Pinnock's that suggests an approach compatible with Clarke's method. Comparing their approaches to the Bible plays a key role in assessing Clarke's congruity with postconservatism.

Clarke's view of the Bible is challenging because he affirmed no theory of the mode of biblical inspiration (Garrett, 1974:186). The question to be answered is whether or not his description of revelation and inspiration is compatible with a contemporary postconservative view. While an exact equivalence would not be necessary to establish Clarke as a postconservative precursor, a close equivalence should be evident. Also important in making this determination is the evaluation of Clarke's view of the central inspiration passage of the New Testament, 2 Timothy 3:15-17. For this purpose, Goodrick's (1982) exegetical study of 2 Timothy 3:16 and Garrett's (1974:187-190) treatment of Clarke's view of inspiration are helpful in comparing the conclusions of Pinnock and Clarke on the subject.

2.4   CONCLUSION

The two most important sources for this study are Olson's (2007) *Reformed and Always Reforming* and Clarke's (1898) *Outline of Christian Theology*. These two works represent the theoretical model and the instrumental case—the two foci around which the study revolves. In addition, Pinnock (1990b), Pinnock and Callen (2006), Goodrick (1982), and Garrett (1974) support the central theoretical argument of the study, and Clarke's (1905, 1920, 1909b) lectures, addresses, and theological autobiography serve to deepen understanding of his *Outline*. The major study by

Howe (1980) is the most valuable secondary source on Clarke followed by the shorter summaries of his theology by Tull (1972), Dorrien (2003), Garrett (2009), and Reist (1970, 1975).

The literature reviewed thus far provides more than adequate resources to meet the objectives of the study. The analysis of Clarke's experiential theology and *Outline* are aided, not only by the primary and secondary sources that explain it, but by Clarke's own clear, literate and non-technical style (objectives 1-2). Clarke comes as close to writing a homiletical theology as does Calvin (2008) in his *Institutes*, and Clarke's more popular style does not sacrifice precision in his formulations. Postconservatism is also well supported by precise and authoritative sources that facilitate comparison, contrast, and evaluation in relation to Clarke (objective 3). The fourth objective regarding the movement from *Dogmatik* to *Glaubenslehre* requires sources providing adequate historical context and definition, so quality—not quantity—is the important consideration.

At this point, it would be appropriate to consider either the theoretical model (postconservatism) or the instrumental case (Clarke). Because Clarke is the primary focus of the study, elaborating his experiential theology takes first priority. Therefore, the following chapter will consider Clarke's epistemological and theological methods before analyzing the Christian doctrines of the *Outline*.

3.0 CLARKE'S EXPERIENTIAL THEOLOGY

3.1 INTRODUCTION

William Newton Clarke was born in Cazenovia, New York, the second son and the third of four children of Baptist minister, William Clarke. His father and mother, Urania, were devoted to the Bible and to the Baptist tradition. He was educated at the Oneida Conference Seminary (Cazenovia, New York), Madison University (Hamilton, New York), and graduated from the Hamilton Theological Seminary in 1863. He pastored three Baptist congregations until 1883, at which time he accepted the Professorship of New Testament Interpretation at the Baptist Theological College of Toronto. This decision was prompted by a fall that winter that permanently injured his left knee, making pastoral work difficult. Despite another fall the following year that left his right elbow permanently injured (he was forced to learn to write with his left hand), he returned to pastoral work in 1897, accepting his last pastorate at the Newton Centre Church in Hamilton. In 1890, his former theology professor, Ebenezer Dodge, died suddenly, and Clarke was asked to temporarily fill his post at the Hamilton Seminary. By the end of that academic year, Clarke was offered and accepted the Joslin Professorship of Christian Theology (Howe, 1980:4-22; Clarke, 1916:1-64; Dorrien, 2003:31-36).

Clarke viewed himself preeminently as a preacher and an exegete. While teaching the New Testament in Toronto, he had been grateful that he did not have to teach theology (Clarke, 1916:64-65). While such a post was never sought or desired by Clarke, his progressive temperament combined with an exceptional gift for explaining complex theological ideas fit him for a work he had never envisioned. In Clarke's first Fall term at Hamilton Seminary, the supply of his former teacher's textbook ran out, and he was compelled to find another text or to write his own. He decided he "must do his own work in his own way," and his *Outline* began to "take shape in his mind" as he taught the course in theology (1916:65). A "wholly rewritten" version was printed but not published in 1894, and a final revision of the work was published in 1898 by Scribner's and was immediately successful in America and England (1916:69-70). Being a homiletic theology as well as a systematic theology, the *Outline* reflects the same pastoral qualities as the first Reformation systematic theology by Melanchthon (1521): *Loci Communes*. Frank Hugh Foster (1969:145) called it "one of the great books of the time" (quoted by Howe, 1980:28).

3.2   CLARKE'S EPISTEMOLOGICAL METHOD

3.2.1   PROOF AS RECOGNITION

The best place to begin with any great theologian is the epistemology that undergirds the theological system. As it turns out, Clarke (1909a:56) presented his theory of knowledge in one concise passage from his work that explains the entire system and therefore warrants quotation:

> The Christian doctrine of God does not begin with proof, it begins with the announcement that is made by Christian faith in the pursuance of the Christian revelation. Faith does not set out to find an unknown God, or to assure itself that God exists: it has heard his voice, and begins in confidence in his reality. It assumes the existence of God as its first certainty, and then proceeds to learn about him all that can be learned. The Christian doctrine is reached by unfolding the conception of God that is assumed as true by the Chris-

tian revelation and experience. When the doctrine has been presented, and it is apparent what manner of God the Christian faith is assuming to exist, it will be time to inquire how far the doctrine thus obtained is commended as true by fitting in with other truth that we have reason for holding. Proof comes at the end, not at the beginning and bears the nature of confirmation, not of discovery. There may be other ways of approaching the knowledge of God, but the Christian way is the way of recognition rather than of demonstration.

The entirety of Clarke's method is revealed here and anticipates the presuppositional approach that came after him with an important difference: Clarke's method is experiential, whereas later presuppositionalism is transcendental (cf. Frame, 2006). Consistent with the Bible's emphasis on revelation in nature and in Christ (PSA 19; ROM 1:19-20; ACT 17:30-31), Clarke argues from the experience of God to supportive proofs that confirm what is recognized as Christian truth. While transcendental and traditional arguments may rationalize Christian experience, such arguments are not demonstrations or foundations of belief, but all are valuable as confirmations of the God recognized in Christian experience (cf. Clarke, 1898:102-128, 104; 1899a:158-159; 1905:65).

3.2.2 TRUTH AS CORRESPONDENCE

An experiential theology of recognition is open to the torsion of subjectivism—a torsion that bends but does not break Clarke's theology. Christian experience and its confirmation through evidence and argument has truth for its object, and Clarke (1898:383) defines truth in terms of correspondence: Truth is "that which accords with reality;

it is that which really is." Clarke reflects a commitment to the epistemological realism of his time but had no illusions of "unfailing correctness" or of complete truth in any area (1898:384). Progress is to be pursued and expected in every area of endeavor under the guidance of the Holy Spirit who leads the trusting seeker into fresh expressions of truth.

3.3 CLARKE'S EXPERIENTIAL METHOD

3.3.1 CHRISTIAN EXPERIENCE AND THEOLOGY

The experiential cast of Clarke's theology is evident in this epistemology. Rather than seeking to establish truth outside the subjectivity of the individual, he sees the revelation of God as addressing the individual through the personal faculties of a divine image bearer. Like Kierkegaard, Clarke believed that religion is inescapably a matter of the human heart and life, and truth is never captured in mere propositions or demonstrations. As Tull (1972:160) observed, "Clarke resembled Schleiermacher" in this respect. Because theology is "preceded by religion," the subjectivity of knowing God in Christ is central to his method. Unlike Schleiermacher, however, Clarke believed religious experience is determined by Christian revelation, not the neutral God-consciousness of a particular time (Pinnock, 1990b:99-102, 186).

Christian revelation and the natural world provide the sources for theology, and Christian experience mediates between theology and its sources (Clarke, 1898:10-53). While this seems a radical claim, it is actually self-evident from Clarke's point of view. The Christian must read God's revelation wherever it is found and interpret it by the leading and illumination of the Holy Spirit. The revelation of Christ "has to be carried to the inner life and made real in experience" (Tull, 1972:161). There is simply no pre-interpreted revelation in nature or Scripture to which the

Christian may appeal as a neutral deposit of truth. The Bible itself is an expression of religious experience that only lives on in Christ's disciples today because Christ begets the same experience in them that the first disciples shared (Clarke, 1898:18). Christian experience, however, is not exactly the same in every age, since the spiritual environment changes, and the Scriptures are interpreted afresh according to the progress and opportunities of each new movement of church history. In a concise summary, Clarke (1909b:210) writes, "a system of theology has God for its centre, the spirit of Jesus for its organizing principle, and congenial truth from within the Bible and from without for its material."

3.3.2 THE BIBLE AND THEOLOGY

The Bible, then, is not simply a repository of doctrines to be mined over and over again as the Church reprises a static theology for new audiences. Rather, the Scriptures are themselves a derivative product of revelation and religious experience, a servant and not a master (Clarke, 1898:21). Because Christianity is a "life-religion," it may not be reduced to a "book-religion." By the 1870's, Clarke's (1898:40) mature reading of Scripture led him to view the biblical writers as inspired and the writings to be inspired in a "secondary" sense (cf. Grenz, 1993:133). He advocated no theory of biblical inspiration, recognizing different degrees of inspiration within the canon depending on content and circumstance. While rejecting a verbal theory entailing inerrancy, Clarke (1898:35-47) would likely have agreed with Beegle's (1963:136-137) view of "varieties of inspiration." Regarding "intuition, illumination, dictation, and dynamic views of inspiration," Beegle believed it probable that all four varieties account for Scripture, and the interpreter simply cannot discern which variety is evident in any single case. The Bible may contain moral difficulties, such as imprecatory psalms that fall below Christ's attitude toward enemies, and minor factual errors based on the authors' limitations, but the Christian teaching of both testaments—correctly discerned—is true and trustworthy. For Clarke, the Bible is not without error, but the Christian teaching it contains is certainly true and free from error. Biblical criticism may expose moral difficulties and factual discrepancies, but it does not undermine clear and coherent Christian teaching that may conflict with the spirit of an age. Christ is the highest revelation and therefore the criterion of the "revelational quality" of the Bible (Tull, 1972:163). Put simply, Christian teaching is the Canon within the canon of Scripture, and every Christian appropriates the Canon in a personal way. Clarke (1909b:24, 25) calls this Canon "my personal Bible": "All Christians gather out of their personal Bibles to feed upon, all smaller than the great book, and for them more available." This is not a pick-and-choose method, since the Bible contains a coherent Christian theology that may be distilled from its contents (cf. Garrett, 2009:306).

The formation of the canon of Scripture also reflects Clarke's epistemology of recognition. The quality of the writings of Scripture persuaded the church of the divine element in them, despite their unequal quality: "The canon did not make Scripture, but Scripture made the canon." (Clarke, 1898:44). This point is profoundly important because it undercuts any notion of an ecclesiastical or creedal magisterium as an external guarantee of the Bible's inspiration and the church's canon. The Bible's authority proceeds from God by the Holy Spirit, and therefore it cannot be authenticated within the human heart on the basis of human authority. All external guarantees of infallibility within the Church or its creeds are contrary to the experiential dynamics of the Christian faith. Neither the canon nor the interpretation of Christian truth require infallibility in order to establish God's authority within the Church and the believer. Clarke (1909b:160) offers a warning to conservative evangelicals who share the Roman Church's desire for an infallible external authority: "There is no good answer to the claim of the Roman Catholic Church that an infallible standard of belief requires an infallible interpreter."

3.3.3 SCIENCE AND THEOLOGY

If the universe and Christian revelation are sources for theology, then science and philosophy will contribute to Christian truth (Clarke, 1898:50-53). Clarke believed that "all truth is God's truth" wherever it is found and therefore saw no conflict between science and religion: "The newly known universe contributes to theology an enlarged conception of God." (1898:50.) While he accepted the evolutionary worldview that developed in his lifetime, he did not accept it uncritically. Since he believed that the Bible did not reveal the scientific details of the origin of the universe or of humankind, questions in these areas must be remanded to science (1898:222). Philosophy provides a higher perspective than does science and concerns itself with "spiritual meanings" (1898:52). Philosophy is an ally to theology, their perspectives and goals being similar. Biology, physiology, anthropology, psychology, and history all provide support to theology, being vehicles of the revelation of God in nature. Science classifies facts and philosophy spiritualizes them, which makes the sciences, philosophy, and theology "friendly fellow students," each with its own complementary perspective on the truth.

3.4 CLARKE' OUTLINE OF CHRISTIAN THEOLOGY

3.4.1 THE DOCTRINE OF GOD

God is a personal spirit who created humanity in his own image. The infinite personal Spirit reveals himself to finite personal spirits designed to know their Creator primarily through the revelation of his moral character in Jesus Christ. Like knows like, and therefore God's character is best revealed through the incarnation of God in a human person. Christ is "the expression of God" and the "example for men" (Clarke, 1898:78). Through him, God's perfect goodness and holy love are revealed: "We see in Christ what God is and what God does" (Tull, 1972:165). While Clarke discusses the traditional attributes of God, his distinctive emphasis on God's holy love is meant to remove the traditional tension between divine justice and love. Love imparts the good and holiness adheres firmly to it and guides its impartation (Clarke, 1898:72). This holy love is shown especially in Christ's "boundless" desire to seek and save the lost. Christ reveals God's attributes and character. The universe does not reveal God as much as Christ explains the universe. Thus, Clarke's theology is Christocentric without being Christomonist.

Clarke (1898:131-132) affirmed that God is the Creator of the universe, but the method of this work is better understood through science than Scripture. While God's method is "evolutionary," human life may have originated by either a gradual process or by direct creation (Tull, 1972:166-167). The question ultimately depends on evidence, and what matters most is not the answer but the affirmation that all things originate with God. Clarke's view of divine immanence is balanced by an emphasis on divine transcendence and affirms the divine presence in both natural processes and the miraculous. Holy love determines God's methods, and all support human freedom, effectual prayer, and direct providence.

Clarke (1898:161-181) distinguished between an economic Trinity of manifestation and an essential Triunity of three personal and eternal modes of the divine essence. Contrary to Tull (1972:167) who claims that Clarke nowhere affirmed "three distinct centers of consciousness" within the being of God, Clarke (1898:174) clearly affirmed that each of the three persons can be described as "a centre of conscious life and activity." The apostolic church experienced the Trinity as a threefold manifestation and did not question how the three are one. Triunity is a metaphysical conception that developed over time to explain God's inner life. Clarke (1898:177) refers to this position as "speculative, not scriptural," meaning that it explains other Christian teachings, "a mystery that explains many other mysteries" (1898:179). In his last formal statement of the doctrine, Clarke (1909a:241) suggests that the substance category of the Chalcedonian definition created an unnecessary tension in the doctrine of Christ's two natures: "so materialistic a word as substance does partial injustice" to the likeness and compatibility of the two natures. Whereas traditional theology accentuates the difference between deity and humanity in Christ, Clarke's doctrines of divine immanence and the image of God in humanity bring the two natures into a closer unity, thereby making the doctrine more acceptable to intelligent moderns. The problem for Clarke (1898:242) is that no one knows "the substratum of personality, the material, so to speak, in which the personal life is grounded," whereas personality is known by its expressions or manifestations. This adjustment is based on Clarke's (1898:292) pervasive principle that the "divine and the human are essentially more alike than unlike." Thus, the God-Man is known by what he does, not by knowing the essence of his personal constitution (Clarke, 1898:63-181; Garrett, 2009:307; Dorrien, 2003:37).

3.4.2 THE DOCTRINE OF MAN

While human nature shares spiritual and personal qualities with God, it also shares a biological connection to the animal world. Tracing their origin to God by natural processes or special creation, humans may be referred to as sons of God by creation, even though they may lack the filial relationship of the redeemed state and the character of God that comes with it (Clarke, 1898:192; cf. ACT 17:28). Part of the spiritual endowment of human nature is immortality (Clarke, 1898:193-198). This belief is more a matter of experience than "demonstrative evidence," the evidence being "inward, subjective, and more or less indefinable" (1898:193). The divine image combined with the endowment of immortality reflects God's intent that human beings share the goodness and life of their Creator. Personal creatures, however, are free and responsible beings, subject to heredity and environment, which both helps and hinders the moral development of the individual and society. Thus, Clarke was a dichotomist and traducianist (1898:215-221). Human nature is composed of a body and soul, and spirit simply describes the soul in its orientation to God. In addition, the entire being of the person—body and soul—derives from the parents (Clarke, 1898:182-226; Tull, 1972:168-170; Garrett, 2009:307).

3.4.3 THE DOCTRINE OF SIN

Clarke (1898:235) defines sin as "badness," "the placing of self-will or selfishness above the claims of love and duty." Thus, sin is viewed from the standpoint of motive and moral quality. Sin is more than the mere survival of the animal nature, although many sins may be explained this way. Rather, it is the "preference" for and "yielding" to animal appetites over spiritual values that captures the essence of human sinfulness (1898:232). In fact, the development of the higher spiritual life in the human race and the individual (at "responsible age") is what characterizes "genuine humanity" and exposes the domination by animal appetites as abnormal (1898:240). Sin entered the human race "through the early acceptance of evil by the free will of man," but Clarke (1898:239) does not describe the "external conditions" of the Fall. His view anticipates the excellent recent treatment by Walton (2015). Despite the deeply rooted sins of the human race, God will progressively overcome these through a slow and gradual process of the saving work of Christ and the kingdom of God (1898:245). While Tull (172:171) attributes Clarke's "sober optimism" to his "evolutionary presuppositions," it is only fair to say that Clarke was persuaded that God's persistent saving love would accomplish this goal. Evolutionary progress does not explain the spiritual work of God in history.

Clarke (1898:249) defines penalty as "the consequence of sin" and notes that God has "so constituted the universe that sin brings penalty" as a natural consequence. Guilt and punishment are a matter between the individual and God, so neither can be transferred from one individual to another. This point becomes important later in Clarke's view of the atonement. The presence of sin in the world is evident in a morally polluted environment and in hereditary tendencies to specific sins even within families. But sin's penalty is a divine response to individual guilt, freedom, and responsibility. Because God is love, he cannot hate his sinful creatures and therefore looks upon them with a "disapproving love" (1898:258-259; cf. ROM 5:8). What is difficult for humans, however, is possible for God: He can hate the sin while loving the sinner, employing penalty and forgiveness in his moral government of the world (Clarke,

1898:227-259; Tull, 1972:170-171; Garrett, 2009:307;
Dorrien, 2003:37-38).

3.4.4 THE DOCTRINE OF CHRIST

The distinctive focus of Clarke's Christology is his belief
that Christ is the apex of the revelation of God. The Gospels
that present the heart of the Christian teaching are acceptable as an accurate account of the words and deeds of Jesus.
Unlike liberals who were preoccupied with the humanity of
Jesus, Clarke was equally concerned with the revelation of
Christ's deity in the Gospels. He affirmed the "miraculous
birth" of Christ and viewed him as fully human and divine
(Clarke, 1998:263). He interpreted the two natures, as Tull
(1972:172) notes, "not in terms of divine and human sub-
stances, but in terms of the kinship of God and man." Tull
is also careful to note that this kinship is not one of a "pan-
theistic identification of deity and humanity." Again, kinship stresses the spiritual likeness of deity and humanity,
removing the tension of unlikeness that makes the traditional Christology appear "incredible" to many moderns
(Clarke, 1898:290). A common "spiritual constitution" does
not obscure God's unique and greater being (1898:292).
Thus, the Creator-creature distinction is an eternal con-
stant.

The divine-human Christ lived on earth as a single person
with a single will. Through the kenosis, the second person
set aside the omni-attributes of God, but this is not framed
in terms of God's putting off divine attributes but rather of
God's taking on a new redemptive activity subject to human
limitations. As the ideal man, Christ incarnated God's holy
love to deliver the lost from sin to a life of holiness in filial
fellowship with God (Clarke, 1998:277). Clarke speculated
that the incarnation would have occurred even if sin had

never entered the world, the incarnation being the final goal of creation (1898:302-303).

In speaking of the work of Christ, Clarke used the term reconciliation because it addresses the personal breach of fellowship between God and mankind that Christ came to heal. Clarke rejected the legal cast of most atonement theories because they miss the fact that the personal and paternal perspective of the New Testament takes precedence over the legal and the regal perspective of the Old Testament. The barrier to reconciliation is found in mankind, not in God. Theories of debt-payment, law-satisfaction, merit-transfer, or penalty-transfer (Anselm, the Reformers) presuppose a system of meritorious law keeping taught nowhere in the New Testament. According to Clarke, "the method of his saving work is that of grace, which does not wait for anyone's merit or earning, but freely gives" (1898:337). The Son does not satisfy the Father's offended legal demands in his act of saving; rather, the Father and Son are united in the Son's bearing sin in order to save (1898:353). For Clarke, Christ bears the sins of the world that he might bear them away when sinners repent and believe the gospel.

Tull (1972:174) is incorrect in simply identifying Clarke's view as the Moral Influence theory. In his address before the Friends Summer School of Theology at Haverford College, Clarke (1900b:54), specifies his own view as a combination of the Governmental and Moral Influence theories (cf. Garrett, 2009:308; Cochran, 1982:211-212). The Governmental theory affirms that God demonstrates his own righteousness in the sufferings of Christ (Rom 3:25) and may therefore freely forgive. The Moral Influence theory affirms that God through Christ seeks to bring sinners to repentance and faith. Both theories show that "salvation is of God," being "in its motive God's own action." In the other theories, God must "act upon himself in order to influence himself" to save—an idea Clarke calls "self-contradictory or artificial or unreal" (1900b:55). Such theories also falter on the idea that debt, guilt, merit, and penalty are transferable, a conception that undermines grace and forgiveness. Put simply, a debt cancelled through payment by another is not and cannot rightly be called forgiven (Clarke, 1898:260-397).

3.4.5 THE DOCTRINE OF THE HOLY SPIRIT

The Holy Spirit is the third person within the triunity of God, the direct presence of Christ within the redeemed and at work in the world (Clarke, 1898:369-427). Tull (1972:175) adds to this description an eschatological feature that is distinctive to Clarke: "He is also the living Christ returned, for the purpose of carrying on the redemptive mission of Christ in the world." A God who loves the world will be present to the world, especially in those who are called to experience Jesus Christ as a living presence. While Clarke includes no section on the doctrine of the Church within his *Outline*, he covers the heart of this material in his teaching on the Holy Spirit who indwells his people—the Church—and empowers their life and work. As an ecumenical theologian, he was not focused on the institutional church but on the invisible church, the community of saints redeemed and indwelt by the Spirit. The Holy Spirit operates as a convicting presence in the world and as a glorifying, revealing, guiding, and empowering presence of Christ in the saved community (1898:373-389). In saving, the Spirit regenerates and through repentance, faith, justification, and sanctification secures Christ-like character and the holy love of God within the believer (1898:395-418).

Clarke's doctrine of election is grounded and illustrated in the Old Testament, which indicates a selection for service and specific works (Clarke: 1898:389-395). Biblical teaching denies that anyone is chosen "for his own sake and advantage" (1898:393). Election does unite the "two blessings" of salvation and service, but the choice is a call to salvation and obedience that is not rooted in an eternal decree that sets the destinies of individuals. God's desire that all be saved (1TI 2:4) simply disallows a fixed election and reprobation (cf. Spykman, 1981, for a similar non-decretal proposal from within the Reformed tradition). The call to Christian service assumes and requires the call to salvation (cf. 1898:394 on ROM 9-11). On the related topic of perseverance, Clarke (1898:418-424, 418) affirms the permanence of the divine life but not as "an absolute metaphysical impossibility of failure." However, because of God's fatherly perseverance and grace, "God's children all grow up."

3.4.6 THE DOCTRINE OF THINGS TO COME

Clarke's (1898:428-488) eschatology is one of the interesting features of the *Outline* owing to his commitment to a realized eschatology based on the growing awareness in his time of the apocalyptic genre in the Bible. Clarke's (1881:179-195) commentary on the Gospel of Mark reflects a consistently preterist understanding of the Olivet Discourse and its apocalyptic perspective. He held that the New Testament contains two perspectives on the second coming, one apocalyptic and the other spiritual. The synoptic Gospels present the apocalyptic view, which has been misunderstood by the Church due to an unwarranted literalism. By literalizing the apocalyptic language of prophecy the church thinks of Christ as absent rather than present—an error evident especially in the Church's teachings affirming the real presence of Christ in the sacraments and a future visible coming and judgment. The spiritual view of Christ's coming is presented in the Gospel of John

(14-16), which presents Christ's promised return to his disciples after a short absence. This promise is fulfilled on the Day of Pentecost, at the believer's death (JOH 14:1-3), in the judgment that fell on Jerusalem in AD 70, and in the spiritual progress of the kingdom of God. Thus, the Parousia (presence) of Christ is not a future event but an eventful process: "No visible return of Christ to earth is to be expected, but rather the long and steady advance of his spiritual kingdom" (Clarke, 1898:444). This view also shapes Clarke's view of the resurrection.

Resurrection and judgment, like the Parousia, are also ongoing processes in history and not future events (Clarke, 1898:453-466). Clarke (1898:454-455) rejected the traditional idea that Scripture teaches a resurrection or revivification of the mortal body and affirmed that—upon death—each individual is raised and given a body suited to the next world. The analogy between the resurrection body and Christ's glorious body (PHP 3:21) does not require that the believer's body be resuscitated in the manner Christ's was raised. In fact, Paul teaches differently that the "spiritual body" becomes the substitute for the former physical body (1898:455, cf. 1CO 15:35-49). The doctrine of a "resurrection of the flesh" is a Jewish doctrine of the Pharisees, and Paul's view was "distinctly opposite," even though he was trained by them. Judgment, like resurrection, occurs immediately upon death (1898:463, 459-480, cf. HEB 9:27). Christ is the judge, and all are judged by the standard of his holy love—believers and unbelievers alike. The faith of believers is vindicated by their Christ-like love, and unbelievers reflect their faithless lack of Christian transformation through the gospel. The unredeemed continue in another world suited to their condition and under the retribution their sins bring upon them. But even in this state, they are not beyond the possibility of grace and salvation if they turn to the Lord. However, the prospect of postmortem salvation also grows more difficult the longer one continues in sin, so Clarke's brightest hope of future opportunity falls short of universalism (Tull, 1972:176-177; Garrett, 2009:309).

3.5   CONCLUSION

James Tull (1972:178) did not consider Clarke a "profoundly original thinker," and his homiletic style marks him as the popularizer of a mediating theology that he formulated for the first time in the American context (cf. Cochran, 1982:287-288). If originality was not his gift, certainly his "saintly sincerity" and powerful gift as a systematizer of theological ideas warrant the tremendous respect for his work among students and other theologians (Dorrien, 2003:41). Clarke was a synthetic genius, and this explains his impact on American theology. While he does not quote other theologians, it is clear that he read them thoroughly and fully assimilated their ideas. His profound understanding of the underlying connections and systematic implications of theological ideas was on par with the greatest theologians. Not only did he influence other leaders in his own time, such as William Adams Brown, Harry Emerson Fosdick, and Walter Rauschenbusch, but many are unaware of the influence Clarke had on Martin Luther King, Jr. King's theology professor at Crozer Theological Seminary, George W. Davis, had King develop six addresses based on Clarke's *Outline*, most of which are verbatim reproductions of Clarke's theological outlines (Garrow, 1986:7; King, 1992:242-249).

What impresses this researcher after thoughtful consideration of Clarke's work is what Frank Hugh Foster (1969:149) called his "unconquerable conservatism" on issues of Christology (quoted by Handy, 1980:85). It is evident that

Clarke's conservatism extends even further than his Christology. Because he was raised within a conservative environment and progressed to a position that retained the heart of his prior conservative commitments, including Trinitarianism and the virgin birth, Clarke's trajectory is remarkably similar to that of today's postconservative evangelicals, and his experiential method seems appropriate to the evangelical ethos. Some evangelicals, such as Bernard Ramm (1983), would consider Barth a good alternative to conservative evangelicalism. However, Barth was really a postliberal given his roots in 19th Century German theology. The final chapter will explore why Clarke fits better the profile of a postconservative precursor.

4.0 CLARKE AS PRE-POSTCONSERVATIVE

4.1 INTRODUCTION

The aim of this study to establish William Newton Clarke as an instrumental case and postconservative precursor might seem to argue for an arbitrary connection in light of two questions. First, why Clarke and not a better example, such as Lewis French Stearns (1893), who produced a volume similar to Clarke's *Outline* entitled *Present Day Theology*? Cochran (1962:288) notes that this work by Stearns was "earlier, and possibly more able" than Clarke's. But he also notes that Clarke's "outline form and simplicity of expression" were better suited to a textbook to replace the "scholastic" texts of the time than was Stearn's work. Clarke's *Outline* came on the scene "at precisely the right time" and its use for a half-century after his death established its "permanent value" (1962:288-289).

Second, would any current authority on American theology agree that an alignment between Clarke and postconservative evangelicalism makes sense? Dr. Gary Dorrien is Reinhold Niebuhr Professor of Social Ethics at Union Theological Seminary in New York City. Dorrien (1998:185-209, 2003) has published works on both evangelicalism and American liberalism, and his book *The Remaking of Evangelical Theology* has a final chapter on postconservative evangelicalism. As an expert on both Clarke and postconservatism, Dorrien seemed to be the best consultant on the viability of this study and its central theoretical argument. In response to the idea of Clarke as an authentic and relevant resource and precursor of postconservative evangelicalism, Dorrien (2015, 2016) supported the goal of the study and its central argument.

Clarke's established place in American religious history as an exemplary evangelical liberal along with Erickson's

(1997:33) characterization of postconservatism as "part of an evangelical left" seems sufficient in itself to suggest an alignment between Clarke's theology and postconservatism. Combined with Dorrien's supportive comments and the elaboration of Clarke's theology thus far, this researcher is confident that a strong case can be made in favor of the belief that Clarke is an exemplary postconservative precursor. It remains, then to make that case in light of Clarke's theology and postconservative principles.

4.2   CLARKE AS A POSTCONSERVATIVE CASE STUDY

The goal of this instrumental case study is not to defend Clarke's theology or postconservative principles but rather to show their congruity. Therefore, the emphasis thus far has been on clear exposition supported by adequate sources. Given the accurate summary of Clarke's theology, it is now possible to show its alignment with postconservative principles. Postconservatism as a theoretical model is less complicated than Clarke's theology because it is captured in five straightforward principles or hallmarks that have already been stated. At the outset, however, there is one consideration that takes precedence over the five principles in establishing Clarke as a postconservative precursor, namely, that Clarke's personal spiritual journey reflects a postconservative trajectory.

It was noted that Barth is not a good candidate for a post-conservative precursor because his personal journey began within the context of late 19th Century liberalism, not conservative evangelicalism, and therefore reflects a postliberal trajectory. In fact, Barth was a precursor of postliberalism, a movement Dorrien (2001:16) referred to as "essentially a Barthian project." Clarke's (1909b:14, 18) journey, however, began within a conservative evangelical family whose very "existence" was shaped by the Bible; looking back as an adult, he wrote, "No one could believe the Bible more thoroughly than I did." Clarke's (1909b) autobiography of spiritual progress anticipates Clark Pinnock's similar post-conservative biography by Callen (2000), and both reflect similar discoveries, awakenings, and shifts. Clarke (1909a:viii-ix) speaks for both in saying,

> But of course a man is no more bound to agree with his earlier self than with any other man, and I have found myself entirely free to depart from positions that I once held, whenever better light or sounder processes enabled me to do so.

The spiritual journeys of these two men—both Baptists and both New Testament professors who became theologians—are so strikingly similar that it seems obvious that they share the same postconservative trajectory. While Clarke's identification with the hallmarks below is crucial to the argument of this study, his postconservative spiritual journey is the single most important plank in the argument.

4.2.1 CONVERSIONISM

The first hallmark of postconservative evangelicalism refers to "a belief in and spiritual experience of conversion to Christ by faith," which is grounded in a work of God in the life of a person (Olson, 2011:170-172). Evangelicals refer to this as the new birth or regeneration, and it is understood as either a synergistic or monergistic work of God depending on whether faith precedes or follows it (JOH 3:5-7; 1PE 1:3, 23). While having "no definite formula or outward expression," the new birth involves an appeal to a new and transformed life in Jesus Christ by the Holy Spirit in response to repentant faith in Christ as God and Savior (2011:171). Conversion marks "a definite turning point" or "personal decision" in a person's life, but it may come gradually and quietly or suddenly and emotionally. Evangelicals of all types "experience these beliefs and believe these experiences" (2011:172). Clarke (1898:395-409) speaks for himself concerning his commitment to this hallmark; his section on "The Beginning of the Divine Life" is an extensive elaboration of this same understanding of conversion.

4.2.2 BIBLICISM

The second hallmark of postconservative evangelicalism refers to a commitment to the authority of the Bible "in all matters of Christian faith and life" (Olson, 2011:172-173). As the evangelical's "source and norm for everything spiritual," the Bible is not just highly regarded, but it is especially loved and therefore obeyed. While the issue of biblical inerrancy has never been settled among evangelicals, all agree that the Bible is infallible if not inerrant. In referring to the Bible as a "source and norm," evangelicals do not mean that it is the only source and norm; most refer to secondary sources and norms for theology, such as tradition and reason, but Scripture occupies the primary position (Olson, 2007:45-46; Pinnock, 1990b:119; Bloesch, 1978:57-64).

Clarke (1898:10-20) defines the Christian revelation as the self-revelation of God, the manifestation of the person and work of Christ in the experience of God's people and in the Scriptures. The "individual and collective" experience of the Church since the time of Christ "has been the great preserver of the Christian revelation" (1898:18). While the Christian revelation is recorded in the living faith of the Church as well as in the Scriptures, the Christian experience is the internal expression of what the Scriptures preserve as an external record (1898:16). They are two sides of the same coin, not two opposing sources. Thus, Clarke affirms an evangelical Biblicism, but not one that places scriptural propositions in tension with Christian experience. Personal experience also plays into this: "though a theologian is a child of his age, still each one is himself . . . which must necessarily color his thinking about God and man" (1898:19). Despite a more nuanced position that avoids prioritizing sources of theology in terms of a scale of reliability, Clarke may nevertheless lay claim to this hallmark. Veridical Christian experience—in the Church and in the individual—will agree with veridical Christian teaching in the Bible, since all sources must submit to theology's ultimate "first source," Jesus Christ (1898:12). The Bible's Christian teaching is never submitted to an authority or magisterium outside itself, since it communicates God's authority in all matters of Christian faith and life.

4.2.3 CRUCICENTRISM

The third hallmark of postconservative evangelicalism refers to "piety centered on Jesus Christ and his atoning death" (Olson, 2011:173-175). Central to evangelicalism is the gospel of Jesus Christ and his death, burial, and resurrection "as the way to reconciliation between God and the world" (2011:174; 1Co 15:1-7). While evangelicals have continued to disagree on the extent of Christ's atonement and how it works, they agree—according to Olson—that it is "more than a moral example" (2011:175). It is a necessary sacrifice for sins that opens the way to acceptance with God. While Clarke's (1900b:52-53) view of the atonement includes the Moral Influence theory, this is combined with the Governmental theory, which Clarke viewed as an extension of the Moral Influence theory (Cochran, 1962:211-212). If there were really no fundamental difference between these two theories—and Clarke may be read this way—then why did he think it necessary to include the vindication of God's righteousness as a requirement for his reconciliation with sinful humanity? It must be granted that Clarke did

not see this in terms of legal satisfaction, as most governmental theorists do, because he viewed the relationship
between God and mankind in personal and vital terms, not
legal terms. But God need not be under a legal necessity of
his nature in order to be under a moral necessity. Even a
vital and personal relationship requires the maintenance of
the moral integrity of the parties, so the divine acceptance
of Christ's suffering in place of the sinner's punishment
may be understood as a requirement of personal integrity
on God's part: "The twofold object . . . was to win men and
to satisfy God" (Clarke, 1898:339; quoted by Foster,
1969:154). To be consistent with himself and to pass Olson's test for crucicentrism, Clarke must replace legal
satisfaction with a moral satisfaction idea, which is admittedly a subtle twist on the Governmental theory.

4.2.4 ACTIVISM

The fourth hallmark of postconservative evangelicalism
refers to evangelism and social transformation as means of
seeking the kingdom of God (Olson, 2011:175). This is more
than a spiritual goal; it encompasses the social order, even
if it does not seek the Christianization of society. Authentic
evangelicalism must seek more than the salvation of individual souls; it must take "action in the world for the cause
of Christ." This hallmark would appear to be Clarke's
strongest given the fact that his eschatology was focused on
the progressive coming of Christ's kingdom in the world.
Many are unaware that Clarke played a significant role in
the Social Gospel movement. While this has not been the
focus of the study, Cochran (1962:223-285) devotes the last
two chapters of his dissertation on Clarke to this topic in
relation to Clarke's eschatology. Clarke was a member of
the Brotherhood of the Kingdom, a group of Baptist minis-
ters and theologians attempting to bring Jesus' teachings
on the kingdom of God to bear on social movements of the

time. The group apparently convened from 1893 to 1915, and Walter Rauschenbusch was their primary spokesman (1962:247-255). Clarke's (1898:444) commitment to the "long steady advance" of Christ's kingdom was more than a commitment to evangelical activism; it was an assurance grounded in his eschatology.

4.2.5 RESPECT FOR HISTORIC ORTHODOXY

While conservative evangelicals prefer to define the movement primarily by a specific doctrinal content, Grenz (1993:23) and Olson (2011:176) recognize a "convertive" or "conversional" piety as the primary distinctive of evangelicalism. Doctrine is certainly important, as is the "hard-won doctrinal orthodoxy" of the church fathers and Reformers. The main problem with historic orthodoxy, however, is not giving assent to traditional doctrines as much as it is the variations of interpretation within these doctrines. Olson (2011:177) uses as examples the "kenotic theory" of the humanity and deity of Christ and the doctrine of the two natures of Christ. Is the interpretation that Christ set aside the omni-attributes by his incarnation compatible with evangelicalism? Does belief in the deity and humanity of Christ require the Chalcedonian doctrine of two *distinct* natures in hypostatic union? (cf. Leigh, 1981; cited by Olson, 2011:177.) Questions like these complicate any attempt to define evangelicalism in terms of a specific doctrinal standard. Furthermore, the freedom to question historic doctrinal formulations seems necessary to justify the Reformers and other evangelicals who have rightly questioned the status quo in favor of more biblical interpretations of Scripture. Postconservatism, then, is really a liberal conservatism, the word *liberal* referring to the freedom to reexamine traditional formulations from a respectful but unslavish commitment to the Great Tradition of Christian theology.

This hallmark—like the previous one—seems most clearly represented by Clarke. His respect for the Great Tradition of Christian orthodoxy is unmistakable in his commitment to the Trinity, the virgin birth, the resurrection of Christ, and justification through faith alone. And yet, his *Outline* reflects modest theological revisioning within his Bibliology, Christology, soteriology, and eschatology especially. In this researcher's view, these revisions do not constitute departures from the Great Tradition that warrant placing Clarke outside of orthodoxy or evangelicalism. In fact, he seems to be a paradigm case of liberal conservatism in the best sense. While his commitment to the Higher Criticism of his time and a late shift with respect to the Trinity are not without fault and will be addressed below, it is clear that he avoided the naturalism and historicism of the German liberals and affirmed an authentic Christian supernaturalism. Given Clarke's congruence with postconservative principles, then, this researcher would consider the central theoretical argument to be sound: William Newton Clarke remains an authentic and relevant resource for postconservative evangelicals.

4.3   FROM DOGMATIK TO GLAUBENSLEHRE

Given that Clarke negotiated the theological crisis of the 19th Century in the American context, it will be helpful to determine where he fits with respect to the momentous changes that took place during his lifetime. If he is legitimately regarded as a postconservative precursor, knowing where he fits also provides insight into where today's postconservatives fit within a two-century context. If the alignment between Clarke and postconservatives has been successfully argued, then Clarke's problems, challenges, and pitfalls are also those of contemporary postconservatives. The central issue of Protestant theology in the 19th Century, in this researcher's judgment, is that of the nature of theology, first as it was understood during the Reformation and then as it was transformed by Schleiermacher and Troeltsch. While a concise summary of this issue is challenging, Gerrish's (1993) explanation of the movement of modern theology from *Dogmatik* to *Glaubenslehre* combined with Allen's (1980) elaboration of Troeltsch's role in that movement should enable the task. No more will be attempted than to explain the movement and to position Clarke and postconservatism with respect to it.

4.3.1   THE OLD PROTESTANTISM OR THE NEW

Gerrish (1993:239-240) distinguishes the old Protestantism of the Reformers from the new Protestantism of the 19th Century German theologians by two different views of the nature of theology. For the Reformers, theology is *Dogmatik*: Doctrines are distilled from biblical propositions and organized into an essentially deductive system of Christian beliefs or dogmas. For Schleiermacher and Troeltsch, theology is *Glaubenslehre*: Doctrines are derived from an inductive and historical study of the changing beliefs of the Christian community, and thus there are no "definitive *forms* of faith"—no dogmas. By the time the new Protestantism reaches its apex in Troeltsch, the Bible and theology are radically historicized, which reduces or eliminates supernaturalism in the Bible and in Christian experience. Thus, historicism tends toward naturalism. The history of doctrine, then, becomes a "ceaseless flux" in which no "fixed or final points" may be identified, and Protestantism is simply "a new expression of the Christian spirit" (1993:242). From Troeltsch's historicist perspective, the two Protestantisms are antithetical (1993:243; Allen, 1980:40). Theology does not reflect the harmony of the Bible and Christian experience; rather, it reflects the harmony of the historical and psychological viewpoints relative to Christian believing.

Troeltsch believed that the new Protestantism was linked to the old through Martin Luther's *sola fide*, which he took to mean that "religion is drawn entirely into the domain of the psychologically transparent" (Gerrish, 1993:244). Gerrish (1993:246) partly agrees with Troeltsch, recognizing that Luther did make "the believing subject the object of thought," which was Schleiermacher's concept of *Glaubenslehre*. But does this mean, then, that all dogmatic propositions are merely "a personal religious confession"? (Allen, 1980:51.) This depends, of course, on whether one grants the historicism of the new Protestantism. If one rejects it, then it is possible, as Gerrish (1993:246) says, to "make the religious subject the object of inquiry without making either the inquiry or the religion subjective." The effect of the Higher Criticism of Schleiermacher and Troeltsch was to isolate the theologian within the Christian consciousness of a specific time, making it impossible to connect with the Word of God in the way the Reformers believed this was possible. Once the Bible is swallowed up in this historicist subjectivity, it is no longer possible to speak of a true Christian theology.

4.3.2   THE OLD PROTESTANTISM AND THE NEW

The key question on this issue is whether or not Luther's faith in Scripture made him sovereign over it, eliminating any possibility for true Christian doctrines that speak with divine authority (Gerrish, 1993:247). The answer to this question determines whether there has actually been a movement in theology from *Dogmatik* to *Glaubenslehre* or merely the realization of a psychological transparency that need not swamp Protestant theology in subjectivism. In fact, the movement from the old Protestantism to the new may be understood in terms of an addition rather than a replacement. If one approaches the theology of Clarke and postconservatism with this in mind, it is evident that theology is—and must be—both *Dogmatik* and *Glaubenslehre*, both scriptural and an expression of the Christian consciousness at a particular time. Viewed in this way, the theologian may critique the weakness of each method from the perspective of the other, recognizing that both perspectives are necessary for a theology in which infallible Christian truth mirrors vital Christian experience. Both Clarke and postconservatism reflect an old and new Protestantism but reject the rationalistic objectivism of the old and the relativistic subjectivism of the new.

4.4   FINE-TUNING CLARKE'S POSTCONSERVATISM

The study of Clarke's experiential theology raised three issues of personal concern that touch the stability and consistency of his system. While these are not the only problematic issues, they are the three most relevant to this researcher: (1) A problem of instability at the heart of Clarke's doctrine of Scripture; (2) An apparent inconsistency in his commitment to immortal soulism; (3) A later shift regarding his doctrine of divine Triunity.

4.4.1   CLARKE'S BIBLIOLOGY

It was noted above that the torsion of subjectivism bends but does not break the experiential theology of Clarke's *Outline*. The twisting pressures of subjectivism are evident in Protestant theology throughout the 19th Century beginning with Schleiermacher and reaching their apex in Troeltsch (Allen, 1980). Therefore, this same pressure on Clarke should not be ignored, and an honest appraisal of the impact of subjectivism on his theology reveals a problem: The ability to discern infallible Christian teaching within a fallible record is compromised by Clarke's insufficiently critical acceptance of the Higher Criticism. This researcher would contend that without an adjustment to Clarke's theology at this point, his doctrine of Scripture is not stable enough to prevent defections from the conservative truths he defended.

Clarke (1898:36) affirms the following as the probable translation of 2 Timothy 3:16: "'Every inspired scripture,' or writing, 'is profitable.'" He goes on to affirm that there "is no authority in the Scriptures for applying the verse to the Bible as a whole" since it refers to the Old Testament. Nevertheless, all canonical Scripture gives evidence of the quality of inspiration, albeit unequally (1898:44). Thus, Clarke affirms what might be called a consubstantial view of plenary inspiration: The divine influence exercised primarily on the authors may be recognized in, with, and under their writings (cf. Garrett, 1974:187-190; Grenz, 1993:120-121; Goodrick, 1982:484, "God breathes into the Scripture"). Their sacred content conveys their authority, not by an infallible form of words influencing the intellect from without, but by the Holy Spirit's use of infallible Christian truth from within (1898:45-46). In summary, the abiding Spirit is the infallible guide, not an infallible church or book: "The Holy Spirit is our teacher, and the Bible is his servant, to show us Christ." (1898:47.) This is essentially Robert Barclay's (1991:46-55) Quaker view of inspiration.

The unequal influence of inspiration on the biblical writers and the fallibility of their writings is not necessarily a problem provided that the infallible Christian teaching is readily discernable within the biblical record. The ability to discern infallible teaching within a fallible record—even given the Holy Spirit's guidance—would seem to require a high level of coherence within the Bible and a low level of error. In fact, this is the principle on which all historical study proceeds. Moreover, if Christ is the apex of the revelation of God, then the record of Christ's words and deeds must be generally accurate, allowing for only incidental errors in the transmission of the text and minor discrepancies that may be resolved or trivialized by comparing Scripture with Scripture. It is at this point that Clarke's commitment to the German rationalism of his time destabilizes his doctrine of Scripture.

While he rarely appeals to higher critical theories to solve theological problems, two examples serve as illustrations. First, Clarke (1909b:184-192) struggled with the idea from his early family training that the Old Testament affirmed a merit-based concept of salvation that contradicts the grace-based teaching of the prophets, Christ, and Paul. In order to resolve these two "contradictory" perspectives, Clarke accepted the contention of the Higher Criticism that the developed Jewish legal system, with the exception of its spiritual "rudiments," came into being after the time of the prophets (1909b:189). Second, Clarke (1911b:11, 12) affirmed the "possibility" that some sayings may have crept into the gospels in the historical process that Jesus did not speak. Such sayings would be revealed by their inconsistency with his "characteristic thought." While Clarke was confident that the Christian mind is capable of discerning the truth within such inconsistencies, the principles of the Higher Criticism were logically taken to unorthodox ends by other theologians who went beyond their modest use by Clarke (e.g., Harry Emerson Fosdick and Martin Luther King, Jr.).

While engagement with Higher Criticism is beyond the scope of this study, this researcher would affirm that Clarke's commitment to infallible Christian teaching within the Bible calls the Higher Criticism into question on grounds that were articulated in his time by Orr (1906, 1980, 2002). Orr (1980:111; 2002:150-151) makes four relevant points against the radical Higher Criticism that bear on the structure of the Bible and the authority of Christ: (1) Much of the Higher Criticism disintegrates the

Bible into conflicting ideas and sources, rather than preserving the coherence needed for an unambiguous theology; (2) The foundational history, laws, and personages of Israel are undermined by the affirmation of their post-exilic invention; (3) It strains credibility to believe that the Jews returning from Babylon would have accepted a fabricated history and legal system as the "law of life"; (4) That Jesus made false pronouncements in line with popular beliefs concerning the Old Testament and its teachings is a "perilous assertion" and misapplies the limits of his human knowledge (cf. Wenham, 1994). Interestingly, when Jesus affirms that the Scripture cannot be "broken" (JOH 10:35), the original word means "'to destroy,' 'to break up,' 'to invalidate'" (Büchsel, 1985:544). By disintegrating or breaking up the biblical record, its teachings are easily invalidated or "set aside" (Bible, 1972; cf. Dorrien, 1998:196). Clarke's confidence in the scientific nature of the biblical criticism of his time led him to overlook its unscriptural naturalist and historicist presuppositions (1998:188; cf. Foster, 1969:100-101, 149). In fact, Jewish and Christian scholars living at the time the sacred writings were published were in a better position to determine introductory matters than modern critics: "It is not easy to wreck a train long after it has gone by. Literary forgeries are soon detected. Whether a book is historical or fictional is recognized on publication." (Halley, 1965:746.)

It is clear to this researcher that Clarke's reliance on Higher Criticism was not necessary to the method and content of his theology. Had he remained committed to the traditional biblical criticism, his theological development would likely have resulted in the same trajectory, including his views on inspiration. Lest it be thought that Clarke's view of Scripture is not up to an evangelical standard—even after discounting his higher critical views—it should be acknowledged that all views of inspiration entailing inerrancy separate content within the Bible, with the possible exception of "absolute" autographic inerrancy (Erickson, 2013:191-193). Even Erickson's "full" inerrancy position requires the acknowledgement that there are erroneous statements in the Bible, even if only reporting "the false statements of ungodly persons" (2013:202). If inerrancy pertains to "what is affirmed or asserted rather than to what is merely reported," it should be clear that even for conservative evangelicals like Erickson, the Bible as a whole is not without error, but rather something within the Bible is so. How is the position of inerrant statements or affirmations within the Bible significantly more orthodox than Clarke's inerrant Christian teaching within the Bible, except that Clarke may be more open to theological developments within the Bible based on progressive revelation? In one sense, Clarke's position has the advantage of being more specific than Erickson's by clearly identifying the inerrant content the Bible affirms. Interestingly, most discussions of biblical inerrancy by evangelicals are not really about the Bible's inerrancy but about an inerrant teaching content within the Bible—not unlike Clarke's Canon within the canon of Scripture (cf. Bloesch, 1978:64-70; Fackre, 1987:71-73, on Essentialist and Christological Infallibility). On this point, Clarke finds himself in the good company of Luther, Robert Barclay, and today's postevangelicals.

4.4.2 IMMORTAL SOULISM

A second adjustment to Clarke's theology could be made with respect to his doctrine of immortal soulism. Clarke (1911a:5) admits that he was raised in an atmosphere "saturated with the thought of immortality." As a young boy on a summer Sunday afternoon, he stood by an open grave holding his father's hand and was "awed by the solemn majesty of death." Suddenly, the minister's voice broke the silence, and Clarke (1911a:6) was "thrilled" by the words of John 11:25: "I am the resurrection and the life." The reality of immortality "was driven deep home" by this experience. Clarke admits that his belief was primarily "influenced by his inheritance," but it was also supported by the "common feeling and thought from immemorial times."

The limitations of this study forbid a detailed refutation of Clarke on this point, but it is feasible to suggest reasons why conditional immortality may fit Clarke's theology better than immortal soulism. The idea that immortality is a gift of salvation rather than a natural endowment of the soul was apparently never a live option in Clarke's mind, despite the following: (1) An eternal aspiration by Christians and humanity at large is no proof of an eternal constitution, especially since "God only has immortality" (Bible, 1982) and Christ "has brought life and immortality to light through the gospel" (1TI 6:16; 2TI 1:10; Pinnock, 1987, 1990a); (2) Clarke's belief that the entire being of the person—body and soul—derives from the parents (traducianism) raises the question of how a process of physical generation results in an immortal soul; (3) Clarke's commitment to a speculative doctrine of postmortem probation is necessitated in part by his immortal soulism; (4) A commitment to conditional immortality would seem to be a better way to balance Clarke's commitment to immediate judgment after death and his distaste for endless retributive punishment (HEB 9:27); (5) Clarke's belief in the holy love of God led to a belief in his endless patience with sinners, but the Bible teaches that divine "longsuffering" has a limit and in judgment God is "a consuming fire" (NAH 1:3; ROM 9:22; HEB 12:29). Again, these reasons offer a perspective that seems a better fit for Clarke's theology, not a refutation of the view he cherished all his life.

4.4.3 THE TRINITY

The final adjustment to Clarke's theology illustrates one of the pitfalls of an experiential theology. It will be recalled that in the *Outline* Clarke (1898:173-174) distinguished between the Trinity of manifestation and the essential Triunity of three eternal modes of the divine essence. His description clearly falls within orthodox parameters. Howe (1980:68) sees the perspective of the *Outline* as "imitative rather than original or unique." Furthermore, he claims that Clarke's efforts "appear to be out of place" in a system that is "frankly based on Christian experience." The evidence of this from Howe's viewpoint is that Clarke "completely abandoned" the approach of the *Outline* in his *Christian Doctrine of God*. In his later work, Clarke (1909a:238) notes that modern theology was "broadening and simplifying the doctrine of God" by recognizing that God is a "single mind and will." In essence, modern theology was progressing to the realization that the church's original conception of God as a Trinity of manifestation was sufficient, leading to the following conclusion: "Without the necessity of differentiations in his Being, the one divine Mind and Will is capable of doing all that has been accounted for by the doctrine of Triunity." (1909a:238-239.)

It was noted above that, for Clarke, Christian experience and biblical teaching are not in opposition, though the Bible may reveal more than is known by experience alone. During the decade after the *Outline*, Clarke (1898:177) obviously concluded that the "speculative" doctrine of Triunity developed by the early Church was not necessarily scriptural, although it was inspired by a certain reading of the New Testament. This researcher believes that Clarke's (1898:175-176) original rationale for the Triunity of God in the *Outline* should not have been forsaken and was—by itself—sufficient to support his first and best formulation:

> Only the doctrine of Triunity affords a so-
> cial conception of God, or adequately satis-
> fies the statement that "God is love." If God
> is love, eternally, not only, it would seem,
> must the impulse of love be in him eternal:
> it would seem also that there must eternal-
> ly be an object fully worthy of his affection.
> But such an object must be as great as him-
> self, and as good.

Howe is simply incorrect in affirming that Clarke's original position was "out of place" in his experiential system. Clarke's original support for the doctrine of Triunity is eminently experiential, for what could be more obvious in experience than that love requires an I-Thou relationship between at least two persons and that such a relationship must exist eternally within the Godhead if God is not just to love but to be love? Clarke's last formulation of the Trinity is admittedly intriguing but not ultimately compelling and sounds a warning against a serious pitfall of his experiential theology.

4.5   CONCLUSION

The experiential theology of William Newton Clarke provides an excellent instrumental case study of postconservative evangelicalism because it illustrates how to be "more evangelical by being less conservative" (Olson, 2007:7). This approach, however, is not without its challenges and pitfalls. Without a stable doctrine of Scripture, the proper subjectivity of an experiential theology can lead to evangelical heart failure through the potentially negative effects of modern biblical criticism. Postconservatives share these same challenges, and its best exemplars reflect—like Clarke—a modest use of modern biblical criticism. As long as the Scriptures and Christian experience remain in sync and harmonious, Jesus Christ may continue to be the

Christian's Teacher (MAT 23:10), and the Bible will continue to be a reliable servant of Christ in preserving and communicating the words of eternal life.

Given the importance of the issue of the Higher Criticism to the critique of Clarke in this study, further research would be focused on the proper use of biblical criticism by evangelicals—both conservatives and postconservatives—since Clarke's time (cf. Orr, 1906; Lewis, 1967; Christensen, 1979; Henry, 1979:383-404; Thiessen, 1979:101-129; Pinnock & Callen, 2006:157-178; Erickson, 2013:92-106). Further research on the roots of Clarke's thinking in the "progressive orthodoxy" of the Andover evangelical liberals would also deepen understanding of his historical context and personal appropriation of these ideas within his own experiential theology (cf. Munger, 1883; Smyth, 1883; The Editors of "The Andover Review", 1886; Foster, 1969; Williams, 1970).

Four personal outcomes of this study have enriched this researcher as a Christian and theologian: First, the study of Clarke's experiential theology has confirmed the belief that his method represents a vital approach that in its essential principles reflects the biblical dynamics of knowing God. Despite its pitfalls, Clarke's method maintains the balance between Christian experience (religion) and its rational expression (theology). Thus, theology may be both *Dogmatik* and *Glaubenslehre*, both biblically coherent and psychologically and historically transparent. Second, the study has also clarified a personal understanding of plenary inspiration that has been many years in the making. A "consubstantial" idea comprising a variety of modes and degrees of inspiration across the canon seems to fit the Bible best, and Clarke's epistemology of "recognition" seems the most honest and defensible way to account for inspiration and canonicity. Third, Clarke's doctrine of the atonement raised an important question that challenged this researcher's own Governmental theory of the atonement: Is the legal-satisfaction idea properly set aside in favor of a moral-satisfaction idea? The central importance of getting the gospel right makes this an urgent question, and the final answer is that Clarke resorted to an unnecessarily subtle distinction. While Clarke's view is orthodox, the moral and legal are closely related in the Bible, and therefore the suffering and death of Christ satisfy a moral demand of God's nature that is also reflected in the legal demand of the Old Testament law.

Finally, the study has enabled a personal resolution concerning the appropriate definition of evangelicalism as postconservative. While terms have no power in themselves, they embody entire perspectives and methods. While Clarke is merely one of many postconservative precursors in his time, he seems to be one of the best, and the study of his theology provided a walk in his shoes on a postconservative path of vital Christian experience.

5.0 REFERENCES

Allen, L. 1980. From Dogmatik to Glaubenslehre: Ernst Troeltsch and the Task of Theology. *Fides et historia*, 12:37-60. Spr.

Barclay, R. 1991 [1678]. The Scriptures. (*In* Freiday, D., *ed. Barclay's Apology in Modern English*. Newburg, OR: The Barclay Press. p. 46-55.)

Beegle, D. 1963. *The Inspiration of Scripture*. Philadelphia: The Westminster Press. 223 p.

Bible. 1972. *The New English Bible*. Cambridge: Cambridge University Press.

Bible. 1982. The Holy Bible: New King James Version. Nashville, TN: Thomas Nelson.

Bloesch, D.G. 1978. *Essentials of Evangelical Theology, Volume 1: God, Authority, and Salvation*. San Francisco: Harper & Row, Publishers. 265 p.

Bloesch, D.G. 1985. A Christological Hermeneutic: Crisis and Conflict in Hermeneutics. (*In* Johnston, R.K., *ed. The Use of the Bible in Theology: Evangelical Options*. Atlanta: John Knox Press. p. 78-102.)

Brown, W.A. 1910. The Theology of William Newton Clarke. *Harvard Theological Review*, 3:167-180. Apr.

Brown, W.A. 1916. An American Theologian. (*In* Clarke, E.S., *William Newton Clarke: A Biography, with Additional Sketches by His Friends and Colleagues*. New York: Charles Scribner's Sons. p. 201-210.)

Büchsel, F. lýō. (*In* Kittel, G. & Friedrich, G., *eds. Theological Dictionary of the New Testament*. Translated and abridged by G.W. Bromiley. Grand Rapids: William B. Eerdmans Publishing Co. p. 544.)

Callen, B.L. 2000. *Clark H. Pinnock: Journey Toward Renewal*. Nappanee, IN: Evangel Publishing House. 293 p.

Calvin, J. 2008 [1559]. *Institutes of the Christian Religion*. Translated from the Latin by H. Beveridge. Peabody, MA: Hendrickson Publishers. 1059 p.

Cauthen, K. 1983 [1962]. *The Impact of American Religious Liberalism*. Washington, D.C.: University Press of America. 290 p.

Christensen, M.J. 1979. *C.S. Lewis on Scripture*. Nashville, TN: Abingdon Press. 120 p.

Clarke, E.S. 1916. *William Newton Clarke: A Biography, with Additional Sketches by His Friends and Colleagues*. New York: Charles Scribner's Sons. 262 p.

Clarke, W.N. 1881. *Commentary on the Gospel of Mark*. Philadelphia: American Baptist Publication Society. 261 p.

Clarke, W.N. 1896. *Mystery in Religion*. (*In* Clarke, W.N. *Immortality: A Study of Belief, and Earlier Addresses*. New Haven: Yale University Press. p. 23-47.)

Clarke, W.N. 1897. *The Circle of Theology: An Introduction to Theological Study*. Cambridge, MA: The University Press. 70 p.

Clarke, W.N. 1898. *An Outline of Christian Theology*. New York: Charles Scribner's Sons. 488 p.

Clarke, W.N. 1899a. *Can I Believe in God the Father?* New York: Charles Scribner's Sons. 215 p.

Clarke, W.N. 1899b. *What Shall We Think of Christianity?* New York: Charles Scribner's Sons. 149 p.

Clarke, W. N. 1900a. *A Study of Christian Missions.* New York: Charles Scribner's Sons. 268 p.

Clarke, W.N. 1900b. The Work of Christ For Our Salvation. (*In* Clarke, W.N. *Immortality: A Study of Belief, and Earlier Addresses.* New Haven: Yale University Press. p. 48-61.)

Clarke, W.N. 1901. Huxley and Phillips Brooks. (*In* Clarke, W.N. *Immortality: A Study of Belief, and Earlier Addresses.* New Haven: Yale University Press. p. 62-85.)

Clarke, W.N. 1903a. Revealed Religion. (*In* Clarke, W.N. *Immortality: A Study of Belief, and Earlier Addresses.* New Haven: Yale University Press. p. 86-107.)

Clarke, W.N. 1903b. The Young Minister's Outlook. (*In* Clarke, W.N. *Immortality: A Study of Belief, and Earlier Addresses.* New Haven: Yale University Press. p. 108-132.)

Clarke, W.N. 1905. *The Use of the Scriptures in Theology.* New York: Charles Scribner's Sons. 170 p.

Clarke, W.N. 1909a. *The Christian Doctrine of God.* New York: Charles Scribner's Sons. 477 p.

Clarke, W.N. 1909b. *Sixty Years With the Bible: A Record of Experience.* New York: Charles Scribner's Sons. 257 p.

Clarke, W.N. 1911a. Immortality: A Study of Belief. (*In* Clarke, W.N. *Immortality: A Study of Belief, and Earlier Addresses.* New Haven: Yale University Press. p. 1-22.)

Clarke, W. N. 1911b. *The Ideal of Jesus.* New York: Charles Scribner's Sons. 329 p.

Clarke, W.N. 1920. *Immortality: A Study of Belief, and Earlier Addresses*. New Haven: Yale University Press. 132 p.

Cochran, B.H. 1962. William Newton Clarke: Exponent of the New Theology. Durham, NC: Duke University Department of Religion. (Thesis – Ph.D.) 324 p.

Dalton, C.B. 1903. The Theology of William Newton Clarke. *Methodist Review*, 85:388-398. May.

Dorrien, G. 1998. *The Remaking of Evangelical Theology*. Louisville, KY: Westminster John Knox Press. 262 p.

Dorrien, G. 2001. The Origins of Postliberalism: A Third Way in Theology? *The Christian Century*, 118:16-21. Jul.

Dorrien, G. 2003. *The Making of American Liberal Theology: Idealism, Realism, and Modernity, 1900-1950*. Louisville: Westminster John Knox Press. 688 p.

Dorrien, G. 2015. (gdorrien@uts.columbia.edu) 05 Nov. 2015. RE: Your Work on William Newton Clarke. Email to: Sotak, M.H. (msotak@regis.edu).

Dorrien, G. 2016. (gdorrien@uts.columbia.edu) 14 Jan. 2016. RE: Max's Study on William Newton Clarke. Email to: Sotak, M.H. (msotak@regis.edu).

Erickson, M.J. 2013. *Christian Theology*. 3rd ed. Grand Rapids: Baker Academic. 1200 p.

Erickson, M.J. 1997. *The Evangelical Left: Encountering Postconservative Evangelical Theology*. Grand Rapids: Baker Academic. 157 p.

Fackre, G. 1987. *The Christian Story, Volume 2*. Grand Rapids: Wm. B. Eerdmans Publishing Co. 366 p.

Foster, F.H. 1969 [1939]. *The Modern Movement in American Theology: Sketches in the History of American Protestant Thought from the Civil War to the World War*. Freeport, NY: Books for Libraries Press. 219 p.

Frame, J.M. 2006. Transcendental Arguments. (*In* Campbell-Jack, W.C., McGrath, G. & Evans, C.S., *eds*. *New Dictionary of Christian Apologetics*. Downers Grove, IL: InterVarsity Press. p. 716-717.)

Garrett, J.L. 1974. Representative Modern Baptist Understandings of Biblical Inspiration. *Review & Expositor*, 71:179-195. Spr.

Garrett, J.L. 2009. *Baptist Theology: A Four Century Study*. Macon, GA: Mercer University Press. 743 p.

Garrow, D.J. 1986. The Intellectual Development of Martin Luther King, Jr: Influences and Commentaries. *Union Seminary Quarterly Review*, 40:5-20. Jan.

Gerrish, B.A. 1993. *Continuing the Reformation: Essays on Modern Religious Thought*. Chicago: University of Chicago Press. 283 p.

Goodrick, E.W. 1982. Let's Put 2 Timothy 3:16 Back in the Bible. *Journal of the Evangelical Theological Society*, 25:479-487. Dec.

Grandy, G. 2010. Instrumental Case Study. (*In* Mills, A.J., Durepos, G. & Wiebe, E., eds. *Encyclopedia of Case Study Research, Volume 1*. Los Angeles: Sage Publications, Inc. p. 473-475.)

Grenz, S.J. 1993. *Revisioning Evangelical Theology: A Fresh Agenda for the 21st Century*. Downers Grove, IL: InterVarsity Press. 208 p.

Halley, H.H. 1965. *Halley's Bible Handbook: An Abbreviated Commentary*. 24ᵗʰ ed. Grand Rapids: Zondervan. 854 p.

Handy, R.T. 1980. The Ecumenical Vision of William Newton Clarke. *Journal of Ecumenical Studies*, 17:84-93. Spr.

Harvey, V.A. 1964. *A Handbook of Theological Terms*. New York: The Macmillan Company. 253 p.

Henry, C.F. 1979. The Uses and Abuses of Biblical Criticism. (*In* Henry, C.F. *God, Revelation, and Authority, Volume IV: The God Who Speaks and Shows*. Waco, TX: Word Books, Publisher. 674 p.

Howe, C.L. 1963. William Newton Clarke: Systematic Theologian of Theological Liberalism. *Foundations*, 6:123-135. Apr.

Howe, C.L. 1980 [1959]. *The Theology of William Newton Clarke*. New York: Arno Press. 125 p.

King, M.L. 1992. *The Papers of Martin Luther King, Jr., Volume 1: Called to Serve, January 1929-June 1951*. Berkeley: University of California Press. 484 p.

Knox, G.W. 1908. Some Recent Works on Systematic Theology. *Harvard Theological Review*, 1:189-206. Apr.

Leigh, R.W. 1982. Jesus: The One-Natured God-Man. *Christian Scholar's Review*, 11:124-137. Win.

Leith, J.H. 1980. *An Introduction to the Reformed Tradition: A Way of Being the Christian Community*. Atlanta: Westminster John Knox Press. 264 p.

Lewis, C.S. 1967. Modern Theology and Biblical Criticism. (*In* Hooper, W., *ed. Christian Reflections*. Grand Rapids: William B. Eerdmans Publishing Co. p. 152-166.)

Madsen, D. 1992. *Successful Dissertations and Theses: A Guide to Graduate Research from Proposal to Completion*. 2nd ed. San Francisco: Jossey-Bass Publishers. 216 p.

Melanchthon, P. 2007 [1521]. *The Loci Communes of Philip Melanchthon*. Translated from the Latin by C. Hill. Eugene, OR: Wipf & Stock Publishers. 274 p.

Munger, T.T. 1883. *The Freedom of Faith*. Boston: Houghton, Mifflin and Company. 397 p.

NAE. 2009. National Association of Evangelicals: Statement of Faith. http://www.nae.net/about-us/statement-of-faith Date of access: 10 Sep. 2015.

Naselli, A.D. & Hanson, C., *eds*. 2004. *The Spectrum of Evangelicalism*. Grand Rapids: Zondervan. 222 p.

Olson, R.E. 2004. *The Westminster Handbook to Evangelical Theology*. Louisville, KY: Westminster John Knox Press. 328 p.

Olson, R.E. 2007. *Reformed and Always Reforming: The Postconservative Approach to Evangelical Theology*. Grand Rapids: Baker Academic. 247 p.

Olson, R.E. 2011. Postconservative Evangelicalism. (*In* Naselli, A.D. & Hanson, C., eds. *Four Views on the Spectrum of Evangelicalism*. Grand Rapids: Zondervan. p. 161-187.)

Orr, J. 1906. *The Problem of the Old Testament: Considered With Reference to Recent Criticism*. New York: Charles Scribner's Sons. 562 p.

Orr, J. 1980 [1917]. The Holy Scriptures and Modern Negations. (*In* Torrey, R.A. & Dixon, A.C., *eds. The Fundamentals: A Testimony to the Truth.* Grand Rapids: Baker Book House. p. 94-110.)

Orr, J. 2002 [1910]. *Revelation and Inspiration.* Vancouver, B.C.: Regent College Publishing. 224 p.

Pinnock, C.H. 1987. Fire, Then Nothing. *Christianity Today*, 31:40-42 . Mar.

Pinnock, C.H. 1990a. The Destruction of the Finally Impenitent. *Criswell Theological Review*, 4:243-259. Spr.

Pinnock, C.H. 1990b. *Tracking the Maze: Finding our Way through Modern Theology from an Evangelical Perspective.* San Francisco: Harper & Row. 227 p.

Pinnock, C.H. & Callen, B.L. 2006. *The Scripture Principle: Reclaiming the Full Authority of the Bible.* 2nd ed. Grand Rapids: Baker Academic. 288 p.

Ramm, B.L. 1966. *A Handbook of Contemporary Theology.* Grand Rapids: Wm. B. Eerdmans Publishing Co. 141 p.

Ramm, B.L. 1983. *After Fundamentalism: The Future of Evangelical Theology.* San Francisco: Harper & Row, Publishers. 225 p.

Reist, I.W. 1970. Augustus Hopkins Strong and William Newton Clarke: A Study in Nineteenth Century Evolutionary and Eschatological Thought. *Foundations*, 13:26-43. Jan-Mar.

Reist, I.W. 1975. William Newton Clarke: Nineteenth-Century Evolutionary and Eschatological Immanentism. *Foundations*, 18:5-25. Jan-Mar.

Smyth, N. 1883. *Dorner on the Future State: Being a Translation of the Section of His System of Christian Doctrine Comprising the Doctrine of Last Things*. New York: Charles Scribner's Sons. 155 p.

Sotak, M.H. 2008. Bernard Ramm: An Instrumental Case Study in Biblical Apologetics. Denver, CO: Regis University. (Capstone Project – M.A.) 47 p.

Sotak, M.H. 2017. *Evangelical Belief: A Course Guide to Christian Thought*. Denver, CO: Sotakoff Publishing. 474 p.

Spykman, G. 1981. A New Look at Election and Reprobation. (*In* Vander Goot, H., *ed. Life is Religion: Essays in Honor of H. Evan Runner*. St. Catharines: Paideia Press. p. 171-191.)

Stake, R. 1975. *The Art of Case Study Research*. Thousand Oaks, CA: Sage Publications. 175 p.

Stearns, L.F. 1893. *Present Day Theology: A Popular Discussion of Leading Doctrines of the Christian Faith*. New York: Charles Scribner's Sons. 568 p.

The Editors of "The Andover Review". 1886. *Progressive Orthodoxy: A Contribution to the Christian Interpretation of Christian Doctrines*. Boston: Houghton, Mifflin and Company. 258 p.

Theissen, H.C. 1979 [1943]. *Introduction to the New Testament*. Grand Rapids: William B. Eerdmans Publishing Co. 347 p.

Tinsley, C.W. 1917. William Newton Clarke, Theologian—An Appreciation. *Methodist Review*, 99:262-267. Mar.

Tull, J.E. 1972. *Shapers of Baptist Thought*. Valley Forge: Judson Press. 255 p.

Walton, J.H. 2015. *The Lost World of Adam and Eve: Genesis 2-3 and the Human Origins Debate.* Downers Grove, IL: InterVarsity Press. 256 p.

Wenham, J. 1994. *Christ & the Bible.* Grand Rapids: Baker Book House. 222 p.

Williams, D.D. 1970. *The Andover Liberals: A Study in American Theology.* New York: Octagon Books. 203 p.

www.ingramcontent.com/pod-product-compliance
Lightning Source LLC
Chambersburg PA
CBHW071840020426
42331CB00007B/1800